MENTAL HEALTH SUPPORT

LIVING WITH DEPRESSION

by Susan Wroble

San Diego, CA

© 2024 BrightPoint Press
an imprint of ReferencePoint Press, Inc.
Printed in the United States

For more information, contact:
BrightPoint Press
PO Box 27779
San Diego, CA 92198
www.BrightPointPress.com

ALL RIGHTS RESERVED.

No part of this work covered by the copyright hereon may be reproduced or used in any form or by any means—graphic, electronic, or mechanical, including photocopying, recording, taping, web distribution, or information storage retrieval systems—without the written permission of the publisher.

Content Consultant: Caleb Lack, PhD, Professor of Psychology, University of Central Oklahoma

---

LIBRARY OF CONGRESS CATALOGING-IN-PUBLICATION DATA

Names: Wroble, Susan, author.
Title: Living with depression / by Susan Wroble.
Description: San Diego, CA: BrightPoint Press, [2024] | Series: Mental health support | Includes bibliographical references and index. | Audience: Ages 13 | Audience: Grades 7-9
Identifiers: LCCN 2023008694 (print) | LCCN 2023008695 (eBook) | ISBN 9781678206666 (hardcover) | ISBN 9781678206673 (eBook)
Subjects: LCSH: Depression in children--Juvenile literature. | Depression in adolescence--Juvenile literature. | Depression in children--Treatment--Juvenile literature. | Depression in adolescence--Treatment--Juvenile literature.
Classification: LCC RJ506.D4 W76 2024 (print) | LCC RJ506.D4 (eBook) | DDC 618.92/8527--dc23/eng/20230417
LC record available at https://lccn.loc.gov/2023008694
LC eBook record available at https://lccn.loc.gov/2023008695

CONTENTS

AT A GLANCE   4

INTRODUCTION   6
JAYDEN'S STORY

CHAPTER ONE   10
WHAT IS DEPRESSION?

CHAPTER TWO   22
THERAPIES TO TREAT DEPRESSION

CHAPTER THREE   34
MEDICINES TO TREAT DEPRESSION

CHAPTER FOUR   44
OTHER TREATMENTS

Glossary	58
Source Notes	59
For Further Research	60
Index	62
Image Credits	63
About the Author	64

AT A GLANCE

- Depression is a low, sad mood. It lasts for weeks or longer. For young people, the main symptoms may be anger and irritability instead of sadness.

- There are many symptoms of depression. People with depression may no longer want to do the things they like. Headaches, stomachaches, and body aches can all be signs of depression.

- People with depression may experience a change in sleeping habits. Depression can also affect appetite.

- Therapies can treat depression. A common type of therapy is cognitive behavioral therapy (CBT). Therapy helps people develop skills to manage their thoughts and emotions.

- Antidepressants are medications that can treat depression. Selective serotonin reuptake inhibitors (SSRIs) are the most common type.

- Electroconvulsive therapy (ECT) and other brain stimulation therapies can treat depression that has not responded to other treatments.

- Healthy sleeping habits, eating well, and regular exercise can help with depression.

- People with depression are at an increased risk of suicide. They can dial or text 988 to reach the Suicide and Crisis Lifeline.

INTRODUCTION

JAYDEN'S STORY

In middle school, Jayden loved sports. He played soccer and ran track and field. He loved being outside and active. He also enjoyed hanging out with his friends and playing video games.

But starting high school was stressful. Jayden lost interest in things he used to enjoy. He stopped going to soccer practice. It was hard to get up in the mornings. Jayden started missing the first classes of the day.

Jayden had been a good student. But his grades began to fall. His coach was upset with him for quitting the team. Jayden's friends stopped calling him

Someone who is depressed may spend less time with their friends.

A sudden change in school performance can be a sign of a mental health disorder, including depression.

to hang out. Jayden thought about harming himself. That's when he knew he needed help.

Jayden started by telling his parents. They scheduled an appointment with his doctor. The doctor diagnosed Jayden with major depressive disorder (MDD). Jayden began meeting with a mental health therapist. The therapist specialized in cognitive behavioral therapy (CBT).

Working with the therapist was tough at first. But Jayden learned to think about his moods. He started identifying how his thoughts and actions affected how he was feeling. Jayden also made changes to his diet and sleep patterns. He started exercising and rejoined the soccer team. Jayden learned to manage his depression. After a while, he felt like himself again.

1
WHAT IS DEPRESSION?

Depression is a mood disorder characterized by low mood. It is different from sadness. People with depression feel down for a long time. They lose interest in things they used to enjoy. Depression can lead to difficulties sleeping. People may experience a change in appetite. They may think about harming themselves.

Depression can be mild, moderate, or severe. Some people experience only one

Approximately 4.1 million US teens experienced a depressive episode in 2020.

depressive **episode** during their lives.
Others may have multiple episodes.

Movie star Dwayne "The Rock" Johnson has depression. He talked about his experience. He says, "You feel like it's only you. . . . I wish I'd had someone at that time who could just pull me aside and say, 'Hey, it's going to be OK.'"[1]

WHAT CAUSES DEPRESSION?

Many factors increase the risk of depression. They often interact. One factor is stress. Abuse and neglect are strong factors. Bullying also increases

Teens that experience cyberbullying are at a greater risk of developing depression.

the risk for depression. This is a reason why **LGBTQ** students have high rates of depression. Their peers may tease and bully them. Other stressors, such as moving or starting at a new school, can also lead to depression.

Stress can lead to changes in thoughts and behaviors. Repeated stress may cause people to incorrectly believe that life will always be hard. They may think they deserve bad things. These thought patterns can worsen depression. They may lead to behaviors such as pulling away from others. People may try to harm themselves.

DEPRESSION AND THE BRAIN

The hippocampus is a part of the brain that helps store memories. It is connected to the amygdala. This part of the brain processes emotions. Both of these brain parts may be smaller in people with depression. Stress may harm growth in these areas. Treatment may help these parts develop.

Genes also influence how likely it is for depression to develop. Depression tends to run in families. People who have a parent with depression are more likely to develop it themselves.

Other biological factors can lead to depression. Neurotransmitters are chemicals that carry signals in the brain. Serotonin is one type of neurotransmitter. Dopamine and norepinephrine are other types. These chemicals have many roles. They can help regulate mood and maintain focus. Researchers study how these three chemicals may influence depression.

Having a parent with depression is a risk factor for developing depression. But stress and other environmental factors are also important.

People with depression have decreased activity in the prefrontal cortex. This area of the brain is directly behind the forehead. It plays a role in decision-making and social interactions. Scientists are studying this brain region. Reduced activity may cause depression. Or depression may result in less activity.

TYPES OF DEPRESSION

There are several types of depressive disorders. The most common type is major depressive disorder (MDD). People must have a low mood that lasts more than two weeks to be diagnosed. They may feel extremely tired. They may think they are worthless.

Depression can last for a long time. People with persistent depressive disorder

(PDD) experience regular symptoms for at least two years. They may have trouble concentrating. They may feel hopeless.

Some people feel depressed as the seasons change. They may have seasonal affective disorder (SAD). Most people with SAD have low mood during the fall and winter. Shorter days can lead to symptoms of depression. People with winter SAD feel better as the days get longer.

SAD can also occur in the summer. Increased levels of pollen can cause summer SAD. So can high temperatures and humidity.

In the United States, January and February are the most common months to experience seasonal affective disorder.

Girls and women may feel down before the start of their periods. For some, the change in mood is extreme. They may feel tired, anxious, or irritable. Those feelings go away later in the month. Doctors may diagnose them with premenstrual dysphoric disorder (PMDD).

DIAGNOSING DEPRESSION

Doctors and therapists can diagnose depression. They often start with a physical exam. Doctors may order lab tests. This helps rule out other health problems. Some health conditions can cause symptoms similar to depression.

PANDEMIC EFFECTS

The COVID-19 pandemic began in December 2019. It was hard on students. In the first fifteen months, more than 140,000 students lost a parent or caregiver to COVID-19. Depression rates in children doubled. Before the pandemic, about one in eight kids felt depressed. During the pandemic, it was about one in four.

Medical professionals ask children and their parents to fill out questionnaires. The forms ask about symptoms and behaviors. They help doctors know if a patient has depression.

Doctors use a book called the *Diagnostic and Statistical Manual of Mental Disorders* (*DSM*) to make a diagnosis. The *DSM-5* is the latest edition. The *DSM* gives doctors information about symptoms. It helps doctors make the correct mental health diagnosis. Then they can work on a treatment plan.

2
THERAPIES TO TREAT DEPRESSION

Early treatment reduces the risk of future depressive episodes. Therapy is often the first treatment type recommended for children and teens. Therapists help patients change thoughts and behaviors. Patients learn to identify unhelpful thoughts and behaviors. They work to learn coping skills.

Changes in behavior and emotion can reduce symptoms of depression.

There are several types of therapy for depression. Therapy can also be given in different ways. Some people meet with a therapist for one-on-one sessions. Other patients may choose family therapy. This can help build a healthy support

Group therapy can help people with depression feel supported and understood by others.

system. Group therapy is another option.

A group of people meet with a therapist.

Group members are dealing with similar

issues. They share ways to cope. This

can make people feel less alone. Therapy

may be given in person. There are also

virtual options.

CHOOSING A THERAPIST

Choosing the right therapist is important. A therapist should use evidence-based practices. These are methods that have been scientifically proven to help with depression. It is also important that patients feel comfortable speaking to their therapist. Therapists should be understanding. They should not force patients to do something that goes against their personal beliefs.

The singer and songwriter Pink received therapy to treat her depression. She said, "What I love about therapy is that they'll tell you what your blind spots are. Although that's uncomfortable and painful, it gives you something to work with."[2]

COGNITIVE BEHAVIORAL THERAPY

Cognitive behavioral therapy (CBT) is a common type of therapy. It can treat depression and other mental health disorders. CBT helps patients identify negative thought patterns. They learn how these thoughts lead to harmful behavior.

Therapists may ask patients receiving CBT to keep a journal. This can help their patients identify and challenge negative thoughts.

Therapists also help patients find solutions to their struggles.

For example, a student on the soccer team may feel upset that she missed a game-winning goal. She may feel as if she disappointed her teammates. She may begin to think she is not good at the sport. She may believe that she should not be on the team. These negative thoughts may lead her to skip practice. She may stop hanging out with teammates.

CBT can help her realize these thoughts are not true. She learns that it is unrealistic to think she should make every shot. CBT can help her remember other strengths. She can learn to shift her mindset about the sport. Soccer can become a fun way to spend time with friends and stay healthy.

Most patients go to between five and twenty CBT sessions. Severe symptoms may take longer to treat. It takes time and practice to change thoughts and behaviors. Patients will need to do work outside therapy sessions. They practice the skills they have learned.

DIALECTICAL BEHAVIOR THERAPY

Dialectical behavior therapy (DBT) is a type of CBT that focuses on managing emotions. It can be used to treat depression. DBT is often used to help people who self-harm. It is effective at reducing suicidal behavior. Over time patients learn how to feel more in control of their lives.

DBT helps patients feel more in control of their emotions.

One skill that DBT focuses on is mindfulness. This is the state of being aware of one's surroundings. People with depression may feel overwhelmed by their emotions. Mindfulness helps people focus on the present. They think about

Meditation is one way people can practice mindfulness.

what they see and hear. They also take time to identify what they are feeling. They can determine why they feel this way. Taking time to practice mindfulness can prevent harmful behavior.

DBT gives patients the skills they need to handle a crisis. It teaches patients positive coping skills. DBT can also help patients with interpersonal, or relationship, skills. Patients can learn to set boundaries. They can learn how to ask for help.

Therapists also help patients accomplish their goals. They work together so that patients can lead happy and successful lives. Dr. Esme Shaller is a clinical psychologist. She specializes in DBT. She said, "DBT therapists believe that the most caring thing a therapist can do is to help push a client toward their long-term goals."[3]

INTERPERSONAL THERAPY

Changes in relationships can cause a mental health disorder to develop. For example, a loved one may pass away. People may go through a breakup. These stressors may result in new responsibilities. They can lead to depression. Negative relationships can also harm mental health.

Interpersonal therapy (IPT) focuses on ways to improve current relationships. It can reduce the risk of depressive episodes in the future. IPT usually takes twelve to sixteen sessions. Patients think about ways their actions may have hurt others.

Interpersonal therapy can be used to treat depression in teens and children.

Someone who is depressed may pull away from others. They may be irritable. IPT teaches patients to deal with these symptoms. It can also help people cope with grief. People can learn to see things from someone else's perspective.

3
MEDICINES TO TREAT DEPRESSION

Therapy is one way to treat depression. Medication is another. The two can be used together.

Antidepressants are medicines that can treat depression. Doctors and therapists will ask patients about their thoughts and feelings. They may give out a questionnaire.

This lets doctors know which symptoms are causing the most problems. They can select an antidepressant that best treats those symptoms.

Medicine made a big difference for actor Jon Hamm. "Antidepressants help!" he said.

Teenagers taking antidepressants may have an increase in suicidal thoughts. Parents should help monitor side effects.

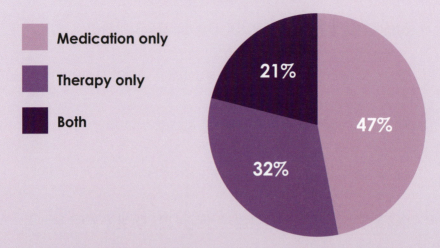

Approximately 7 million US adults received treatment for depression in 2019. Some took medication. Others received therapy. Some adults received both types of treatment.

"If you can change your brain chemistry enough to think: 'I want to get up in the morning; I don't want to sleep until four in the afternoon.'"[4]

There are many types of antidepressants. Doctors and patients work together to find the medicine that is the best fit. Antidepressants do not work for everyone. Sometimes a combination of medicines is necessary. It can take four to eight weeks for these medicines to fully take effect. Doctors often recommend that patients continue taking antidepressants for at least six months after feeling better. This helps prevent depression from returning.

Antidepressants can cause side effects. Some side effects are mild, such as a headache or problems sleeping. Severe

Patients should speak with their doctors if they have concerns about taking an antidepressant.

side effects include an irregular heartbeat. Some studies show that antidepressants can increase suicidal thoughts in children and teens. But untreated depression also increases suicidal risk. It is important that patients understand possible side effects before taking medication. They should speak to their doctor if they want to stop taking a medicine. It can be unsafe to suddenly stop use of some antidepressants.

SSRIs

Selective serotonin reuptake inhibitors (SSRIs) are the most prescribed type of antidepressants. But scientists are still studying exactly how these drugs work. Lexapro and Prozac are two SSRIs. They can be used to treat depression in young people.

SSRIs tend to cause milder side effects than other antidepressants. They are

Some SSRIs can make the effects of caffeine more extreme, so people should limit their caffeine intake.

not **addictive**. But people may feel sick if they suddenly stop using an SSRI. They may feel nauseous and tired. Doctors help patients gradually reduce their **dosage** to avoid these symptoms.

OTHER TYPES OF ANTIDEPRESSANTS

Other antidepressants target different neurotransmitters. Serotonin and norepinephrine reuptake inhibitors (SNRIs) increase serotonin and norepinephrine levels. Monoamine oxidase inhibitors (MAOIs) work differently. They increase the levels of dopamine and norepinephrine.

MAOIs can be dangerous. They are prescribed if other drugs do not work. People who are taking MAOIs need to be mindful of their diets. They should avoid eating foods such as aged cheeses and soy products. These foods can interact

Brain scans may be a way for scientists to determine whether antidepressants are effective in a patient.

with MAOIs. They can cause extremely high blood pressure.

Another group of antidepressants is tricyclic antidepressants. These medicines affect serotonin and norepinephrine. They also influence the levels of other brain chemicals. They can cause more severe side effects than other antidepressants. Because of this, tricyclic antidepressants are prescribed only if other treatments do not work. These medicines can cause drowsiness. People should not drive after taking some types of tricyclic antidepressants.

ATYPICAL ANTIDEPRESSANTS

Atypical antidepressants may be prescribed to treat specific symptoms. They may target different neurotransmitters than SSRIs or SNRIs. Wellbutrin is an example of an atypical antidepressant. Unlike other medicines, it does not affect serotonin. Trazodone is another example. It can treat depression. But it is usually prescribed to help with sleep issues.

4

OTHER TREATMENTS

Medication and therapy do not always help someone with depression. There are other treatment options available. Brain **stimulation** treatments can be used. These treatments may have severe side effects. This is one reason why they are used for treatment-**resistant** depression.

STIMULATING THE BRAIN

Brain stimulation therapies use electricity to activate the brain. Electroconvulsive therapy (ECT) is one type. Patients are given a drug that puts them to sleep. The doctor places electrodes on the person's head.

Patients can talk to their doctors about other ways to treat depression if therapy and medication do not work.

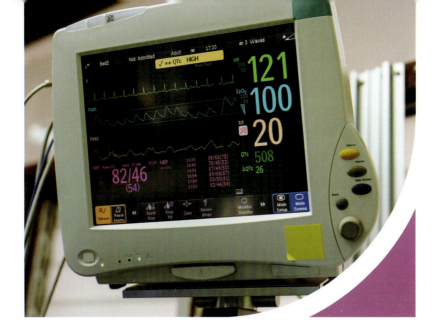

Body functions, including heartbeat and blood pressure, are monitored while receiving ECT.

The electrodes deliver electric shocks to the brain. This helps new cells grow.

ECT works faster than antidepressants. Patients may see improvements after only one treatment. They may not have depressive symptoms within four weeks. Their depression may not return for a long time. But ECT can cause side effects including memory loss. It also requires patients to go to a doctor's office for treatment. Patients receive treatment two or three times a week. They typically receive six to twelve ECT sessions. Each visit lasts for about an hour.

Transcranial magnetic stimulation (TMS) uses a magnet to deliver electric pulses. TMS can target a more specific area of the brain than ECT. Each session lasts thirty minutes to an hour.

The US government approved TMS to treat depression in 2008. Unlike ECT, a patient does not need to be put to sleep to get TMS treatment. TMS also has fewer side effects than ECT.

OTHER TREATMENTS

Some treatments target specific depressive disorders. Light therapy can be used to treat SAD that occurs in the winter. Patients use a light box after waking up. It mimics sunlight. It can help regulate mood. Light therapy can begin working within a few days.

PMDD is typically treated with antidepressants and therapy. But people with PMDD may take medicines that affect

Light therapy has few side effects and can improve symptoms within a week.

hormones too. Hormones are chemicals that influence many bodily functions. Medicines taken for PMDD affect how hormones interact with neurotransmitters.

Doctors should explain possible risks and side effects of medical procedures.

NEW AND CUTTING-EDGE TREATMENTS

Deep brain stimulation (DBS) is typically used to treat movement disorders. Research is being done to see if DBS can also be used to treat depression. Surgery is a part of DBS. Electrodes are placed on specific parts of the brain. Electric shocks regulate activity in these areas. Scientists are looking for ways to deliver shocks only when a person is experiencing symptoms.

LIFESTYLE CHANGES

Lifestyle changes can help with depression. They are not a replacement for therapy or medicine. Healthy sleep habits can improve mood. Adults should get seven to nine hours of sleep each night. Children and teens need even more.

Getting regular sleep may be difficult for someone with depression. People may sleep too much or too little when depressed. But they can take steps to improve their sleep. Therapists can help patients establish a sleep routine. Having a set bedtime and wake time helps ensure quality sleep. People should use their beds only for sleep. For example, studying should

WELLNESS RECOVERY ACTION PLAN (WRAP)

Some mental health centers help patients develop a wellness recovery action plan (WRAP). This is a personalized plan to help with recovery. The WRAP helps patients prepare for their daily lives. They reflect on ways to cope. They have a plan for what to do if symptoms worsen. A WRAP can help people gain confidence. They develop skills that make them feel more in control of their lives.

not be done in bed. Limiting screen time can also improve sleep. People should not use electronic devices half an hour before sleeping.

Exercise can improve sleep. It also has other mental health benefits. It can reduce stress and increase self-esteem. Exercise also causes the brain to release endorphins. These chemicals can improve mood.

Joining a sports team is one way to get more exercise. This also helps people make new friends. Socializing can lead to more mood benefits.

Starting regular exercise can be difficult, but even short walks can improve mental health.

A person's diet can influence mood. People who are depressed may crave unhealthy foods. But foods that are high in fats and sugar can worsen mood. People should instead eat fruits, vegetables, and whole grains. Jessica Bayes does research on how nutrition affects mood. She talked about the effect diet has on depression. "There are lots of reasons why scientifically we think food affects mood," she said. "For example, around 90 percent of serotonin, a chemical that helps us feel happy, is made in our gut."[5]

TALKING ABOUT IT

It can be difficult to talk about depression and mental health. People with depression may face **stigma**. Dr. Thomas Insel treats people with mental illnesses. He says, "We don't understand how common it is [and] how important it is to talk about it. . . . So this is a problem that we all deal with in secret. The result is that we don't deal with it well."[6]

Stigma can make it difficult for people to seek treatment. People may not know who to talk to about mental health. People can find mental health resources online. They can call 988 to reach the Suicide and Crisis Lifeline.

People with depression may feel as if they are alone. But in 2020, 17 percent of US teens reported having a depressive episode in the past year. Therapist Kee

Having a strong support system can help with recovery from depression.

Dunning spoke about how hard fighting depression can be. "You are beyond courageous," she says. "You are stronger than you know. Keep in the fight, stay strong in your resolves, because you are worth it."[7]

GLOSSARY

addictive
causing a dependence or need for a drug or behavior

dosage
a measured amount

episode
a period when a person is experiencing symptoms

genes
units of information that are passed from parent to child that determine traits such as hair and eye color

LGBTQ
lesbian, gay, bisexual, transgender, and queer

resistant
continuing despite treatment

stigma
a societal attitude about a characteristic or behavior that causes people to feel ashamed when associated with it

stimulation
to increase activity or growth

SOURCE NOTES

CHAPTER ONE: WHAT IS DEPRESSION?

1. Quoted in "Celebrity Mental Health Quotes That Will Make You Feel Understood," *Mental Health Center*, October 5, 2017. www.mentalhealthcenter.org.

CHAPTER TWO: THERAPIES TO TREAT DEPRESSION

2. Quoted in Samantha Vincenty, "26 Celebrities Get Real About Depression and Anxiety," *Oprah Daily*, May 3, 2019. www.oprahdaily.com.

3. UC San Francisco, "What Is Dialectical Behavior Therapy for Adolescents (DBT)?" *YouTube*, September 20, 2015. www.youtube.com.

CHAPTER THREE: MEDICINES TO TREAT DEPRESSION

4. Quoted in "Jon Hamm Reveals Battle with Chronic Depression," *Today*, September 12, 2010. www.today.com.

CHAPTER FOUR: OTHER TREATMENTS

5. Quoted in "A Better Diet Helps Beat Depression in Young Men," *UTS*, May 9, 2022. www.uts.edu.au.

6. Quoted in "Hiding in Plain Sight: The Storm," *PBS*, 2023. www.pbs.org.

7. Quoted in "Hiding in Plain Sight: The Storm."

FOR FURTHER RESEARCH

BOOKS

Holly Duhig, *A Book About Depression*. New York: PowerKids Press, 2019.

Christine Honders, *Depression*. New York: Rosen Publishing, 2021.

Cecilia Pinto McCarthy, *What Are Mood Disorders?* San Diego, CA: BrightPoint Press, 2023.

INTERNET SOURCES

"Going to a Therapist," *TeensHealth*, November 2021. https://kidshealth.org.

Robert C. Meisner, "Ketamine for Major Depression: New Tool, New Questions," *Harvard Health Publishing*, May 22, 2019. www.health.harvard.edu.

"Teen Depression: More Than Just Moodiness," *National Institute of Mental Health*, n.d. www.nimh.nih.gov.

WEBSITES

Erika's Lighthouse
www.erikaslighthouse.org

Erika's Lighthouse was founded by parents who lost their daughter to depression. Its goal is to provide resources to teens, families, and schools to "get depression out of the dark."

The Trevor Project
www.thetrevorproject.org

The Trevor Project is the world's largest mental health organization for LGBTQ youth.

The Youth Mental Health Project
https://ymhproject.org

The Youth Mental Health Project educates, empowers, and supports families and communities to better understand and care for the mental health of youth.

INDEX

abuse, 12

brain, 14, 15–17, 36, 42, 44–47, 50–51, 53
bullying, 12–13

cognitive behavioral therapy (CBT), 9, 25–28
COVID-19, 20

deep brain stimulation (DBS), 50–51
Diagnostic and Statistical Manual of Mental Disorders (DSM), 21
dialectical behavior therapy (DBT), 28–31
diet, 9, 41, 54–55

electroconvulsive therapy (ECT), 45–48

genes, 15
group therapy, 24

interpersonal therapy (IPT), 32–33

light therapy, 48

major depressive disorder (MDD), 9, 17
monoamine oxidase inhibitors (MAOIs), 41–42

neurotransmitters, 15, 41, 43, 49
dopamine, 15, 41
norepinephrine, 15, 41–42
serotonin, 15, 39, 41–42, 43, 55

persistent depressive disorder (PDD), 17–18
premenstrual dysphoric disorder (PMDD), 19, 48–49

seasonal affective disorder (SAD), 18, 48
selective serotonin reuptake inhibitors (SSRIs), 39–40, 43
self-harm, 8, 11, 14, 28
serotonin and norepinephrine reuptake inhibitors (SNRIs), 41, 43
side effects, 37–39, 43, 44, 46, 48
sleep, 9, 10, 36–37, 43, 45, 47, 51–53
stress, 6, 12–14, 32, 53

thought patterns, 9, 14, 22, 25, 26–28, 34
transcranial magnetic stimulation (TMS), 47–48
tricyclic antidepressants, 42–43

IMAGE CREDITS

Cover: © marieclaudelemay/iStockphoto

5: © fizkes/Shutterstock Images

7: © Motortion Films/Shutterstock Images

8: © Antonio Guillem/iStockphoto

11: © Prostock-studio/iStockphoto

13: © MachineHeadz/iStockphoto

16: © monkeybusinessimages/iStockphoto

19: © Antonio Guillem/Shutterstock Images

23: © SeventyFour/Shutterstock Images

26: © FG Trade/iStockphoto

29: © VH-studio/Shutterstock Images

30: © Daniel Hoz/Shutterstock Images

33: © Nikodash/iStockphoto

35: © gpointstudio/iStockphoto

36: © Red Line Editorial

38: © FatCamera/iStockphoto

40: © Lyubov Levitskaya/Shutterstock Images

42: © Patrick HeagneyiStockphoto

45: © monkeybusinessimages/iStockphoto

46: © ChaNaWiT/Shutterstock Images

49: © Image Point Fr/Shutterstock Images

50: © Ground Picture/Shutterstock Images

54: © kate_sept2004/iStockphoto

57: © Monkey Business Images/Shutterstock Images

ABOUT THE AUTHOR

Susan Wroble is a Denver-based children's writer who focuses on writing about neurodiversity, STEM topics, and climate change. She also writes for the Colorado Encyclopedia, the Denver Museum of Nature and Science, and the Denver Rose Society. She holds degrees in electrical engineering and foreign affairs and leads Denver's support group for parents of twice-exceptional children (kids who are highly gifted and have learning disabilities). You can often find her volunteering at Colorado Children's Hospital with her therapy dog.